Witness to History

Hiroshima

Nathaniel Harris

H www.heinemann.co.uk/library

Visit our website to find out more information about **Heinemann Library** books.

To order:

☎ Phone 44 (0) 1865 888066

▤ Send a fax to 44 (0) 1865 314091

▯ Visit the Heinemann Bookshop at www.heinemann.co.uk/library to browse our catalogue and order online.

First published in Great Britain by Heinemann Library,
Halley Court, Jordan Hill, Oxford
OX2 8EJ, part of Harcourt Education.

Heinemann is a registered trademark of
Harcourt Education Ltd.

© Harcourt Education Ltd 2004
First published in paperback in 2006
The moral right of the proprietor has been asserted.

Produced for Heinemann by Discovery Books Ltd
Editorial: Nancy Dickmann, Tanvi Rai and
    Patience Coster
Design: Ian Winton
Artwork: Stefan Chabluk
Picture Research: Rachel Tisdale
Production: Séverine Ribierre

Originated by Dot Gradations
Printed and bound in China
by South China Printing Company

ISBN 0 431 17055 X (hardback)
08 07 06 05 04
10 9 8 7 6 5 4 3 2 1

ISBN 0 431 17060 6 (paperback)
09 08 07 06
10 9 8 7 6 5 4 3 2 1

British Library Cataloguing in Publication Data
Harris, Nathaniel, 1937
  Hiroshima. – (Witness to History)
  940.5'425

A full catalogue record for this book is available from
the British Library.

Acknowledgements
The publishers would like to thank the following for
permission to reproduce photographs:
Bettmann/Corbis: pp. 7, 24, 25; Corbis: pp. 5, 6, 13, 14,
15, 16, 18, 20, 21, 28, 32, 34, 46; Popperfoto: pp. 9, 10,
11, 22, 23, 27, 38, 39, 40, 42, 44; Topham Picturepoint:
pp. 29, 30, 48, 49, 50.

Cover photograph shows the destruction caused by the
atomic bomb dropped on Hiroshima in August 1945.
Photo reproduced with permission of Bettmann/Corbis.

The publishers would like to thank Bob Rees, historian
and assistant head teacher, for his assistance in the
preparation of this book.

Every effort has been made to contact copyright
holders of any material reproduced in this book. Any
omissions will be rectified in subsequent printings if
notice is given to the publishers.

Words appearing in the text in bold, **like this**, are explained in the glossary.

All Internet addresses (URLs) given in this book were valid at the time of going to press.
However, due to the dynamic nature of the Internet, some addresses may have changed, or sites
may have changed or ceased to exist since publication. While the author and publisher regret any
inconvenience this may cause readers, no responsibility for any such changes can be accepted by
either the author or the publisher.

Contents

A nuclear strike

During World War II, on 6 August 1945, an American B-29 aircraft dropped a single bomb on the Japanese city of Hiroshima. It was of an entirely new type, and caused terrible destruction, loss of life and injuries. The devastation was on a scale that had seldom been seen before, and then only after many thousands of 'ordinary' bombs had been dropped. A second bomb of the new type, dropped on the city of Nagasaki, forced Japan to surrender. Within a few days, just two super-weapons, known as **atomic bombs**, ended the second major war of the 20th century.

The atomic bomb had been developed in great secrecy, and its effect astonished the world. The bombs were the result of great advances in the science of physics. **Physicists** discovered how to release huge amounts of energy by splitting the **nucleus** (core) of **atomic particles**. That is why the bombs used at Hiroshima and Nagasaki were known as atomic, or atom, bombs. Later, even more fearsome bombs and missiles were developed by splitting or fusing nuclei. Consequently these are all known as nuclear weapons.

How it happened

The atomic bomb was developed during a critical period of 20th-century history. In the 1930s, Germany was ruled by Adolf Hitler and his **Nazi Party**. Hitler's regime was openly ruthless, brutal and bent on conquest. In 1939 the US president, Franklin D. Roosevelt, was warned that German scientists might develop an atomic bomb, and he decided that the USA had to make one first.

Soon afterwards, World War II (1939–45) began in Europe. The USA became involved from December 1941, forming **alliances** with several nations including Great Britain and the **Soviet Union** and making war on Germany, Italy and Japan. Work on an American atomic bomb went on, but Germany and Italy surrendered before it was ready for use. Japan continued to resist fiercely and became the first country to experience a nuclear strike.

The decision to drop the bombs was made by US president Harry S Truman, who took office after Roosevelt's death in April 1945. Historians disagree in their judgements about this decision. Some believe Truman was right, but others think the bombing was unnecessary. Either way, 1945 marked the beginning of 'the nuclear age', when the making of ever more powerful weapons created the possibility that humanity might destroy itself.

Atomic power unleashed: the huge flaming cloud produced by an American nuclear test in the Nevada desert, USA, on 25 May 1953.

How do we know?

Many history books have been written about the events described here – World War II, the making of **atomic bombs**, the destruction caused by dropping them on Japan, and their longer-term effects. Histories of this type, describing great events over quite a long period, are generally reliable and have many uses. They are known as 'secondary sources', because the historian has mainly described things that he or she has not experienced.

However, the pictures of people and events in such histories are mainly based on direct evidence. Most of this comes from 'primary sources' – materials from the time dealt with in the history. These primary sources take many forms. Among them are eyewitness accounts, diaries and letters, records of conferences and meetings, evidence given in courts of law, newsreel footage, and newspaper or broadcast reports by correspondents. In addition, there are documents of many kinds, ranging from deeds of ownership to death certificates. Historians compare and assess all of these sources in an attempt to arrive at the truth.

-2-

The United States has only very poor ores of uranium in moderate quantities. There is some good ore in Canada and the former Czechoslovakia, while the most important source of uranium is Belgian Congo.

In view of this situation you may think it desirable to have some permanent contact maintained between the Administration and the group of physicists working on chain reactions in America. One possible way of achieving this might be for you to entrust with this task a person who has your confidence and who could perhaps serve in an inofficial capacity. His task might comprise the following:

   a) to approach Government Departments, keep them informed of the further development, and put forward recommendations for Government action, giving particular attention to the problem of securing a supply of uranium ore for the United States;

   b) to speed up the experimental work, which is at present being carried on within the limits of the budgets of University laboratories, by providing funds, if such funds be required, through his contacts with private persons who are willing to make contributions for this cause, and perhaps also by obtaining the co-operation of industrial laboratories which have the necessary equipment.

I understand that Germany has actually stopped the sale of uranium from the Czechoslovakian mines which she has taken over. That she should have taken such early action might perhaps be understood on the ground that the son of the German Under-Secretary of State, von Weizsäcker, is attached to the Kaiser-Wilhelm-Institut in Berlin where some of the American work on uranium is now being repeated.

Yours very truly,
A. Einstein
(Albert Einstein)

Part of the letter that led to the USA adopting an atomic bomb programme. The letter was written by the most famous 20th-century scientist, Albert Einstein, to President Roosevelt.

Eyewitnesses

But this is not a simple matter. Primary sources may be misleading in all sorts of ways. They may contain deliberate lies. They may be intentionally or unintentionally biased. Or they may be distorted by ignorance or faulty memory. And there is often such a wealth of sources that the historian has to decide which are the most useful ones. In other words, historians do not just tell a story: they select and interpret their materials. Some topics, like President Truman's decision to use the atomic bomb, are so controversial that historians offer widely different interpretations of them.

This book features the most vivid type of primary source – eyewitness accounts of events. These remind us that history is not just a matter of causes or results, but is experienced by living individuals who do not know how things will turn out. In the story of Hiroshima and the atomic bomb, such people included the **physicists** who worked on **atomic theory**; those who took part in the project to build the bomb; the president who decided that it must be used; the crew of the aircraft that bombed the city; the individuals in Hiroshima who lived to tell the tale; and eyewitnesses of later events. Their stories are both amazing and terrible.

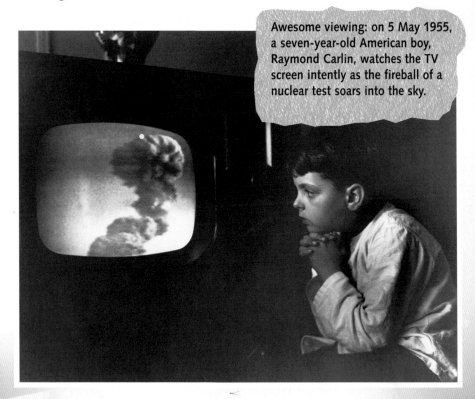

Awesome viewing: on 5 May 1955, a seven-year-old American boy, Raymond Carlin, watches the TV screen intently as the fireball of a nuclear test soars into the sky.

Splitting the atom

An ancient Greek philosopher named Democritus (c.400 BC) was the first person to suggest that all forms of **matter** were made up of tiny particles, or atoms. He believed the atom was the smallest unit in the Universe. Much later, in the 19th century, scientists found evidence that supported Democritus' ideas. Eventually it was established that each atom measured about one ten-thousand-millionth of a metre across.

That, however, was not the end of the story. By the 1930s, **physicists** knew that atoms were not solid but that each consisted of a **nucleus** and the **electrons** that circled round it. Then, in December 1938, two German scientists, Otto Hahn and Fritz Strassman, bombarded **uranium** with particles called **neutrons**. The result puzzled them, and at first they failed to realize that they had split the nucleus of the uranium.

This was the first example of human-engineered **nuclear fission** – 'splitting the atom'. Physicists were wildly excited by the discovery. Most of them were engaged in 'pure' research, with no practical end in view. But some realized that the energy released by the splitting might be used for industrial purposes. And a few saw that it might lead to the creation of a new, awesomely destructive weapon.

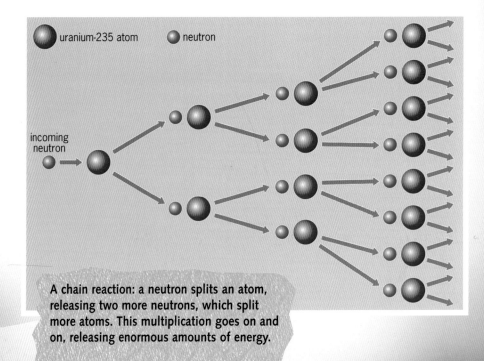

A chain reaction: a neutron splits an atom, releasing two more neutrons, which split more atoms. This multiplication goes on and on, releasing enormous amounts of energy.

The excitement of discovery

Lise Meitner and her nephew Otto Frisch were scientists who had been forced to leave Nazi Germany. Frisch described how they discovered that German physicists had, without realizing it, brought about nuclear fission.

I found Lise Meitner studying a letter from [the scientist, Otto] Hahn and obviously worried by it. I wanted to tell her of a new experiment I was planning, but she wouldn't listen; I had to read that letter. Its content was indeed so startling that I was at first inclined to be sceptical.

Was it just a mistake? No, said Lise Meitner; Hahn was too good a chemist for that. But how could **barium** be formed from [bombarding] uranium [with neutrons]?

Otto Hahn, one of the pioneers of research into atomic energy. He was awarded the 1947 Nobel Prize for chemistry.

At that point we both sat down on a tree trunk . . . and started to calculate on scraps of paper . . . [We concluded that] the uranium nucleus might indeed resemble a very wobbly, unstable drop, ready to divide itself at the slightest provocation, such as the impact of a single neutron.

Whenever **mass** disappears energy is created, according to [the world-famous scientist [Albert] Einstein's formula $E=mc^2$ . . . So here was the source for that energy; it all fitted!

A couple of days later I travelled back to Copenhagen in considerable excitement. I was keen to submit our speculations to [Danish scientist Niels] Bohr, who was just about to leave for the USA. He had only a few minutes for me; but I had hardly begun to tell him when he struck his forehead with his hand and exclaimed: 'Oh, what idiots we all have been! Oh, but this is wonderful!'

Warning the president

Hahn and Strassman, the discoverers of **nuclear fission**, lived in **Nazi** Germany. There, scientists had to do as they were told. Were they already working on a weapon that harnessed the energy released by splitting **uranium** atoms? Leo Szilard, a Hungarian-born scientist working in the USA, thought they might be. The idea that Hitler, a ruthless, power-hungry **dictator**, might possess such a weapon was frightening. Moreover, Szilard's own experiments suggested that it was possible to bombard **nuclei** with **neutrons** and produce yet more neutrons. The process would go on and on, in a chain reaction that would generate huge quantities of explosive energy.

It was not yet certain that an **atomic bomb** was a practical possibility. But Szilard was worried enough to go to see Albert Einstein, the most famous scientist of the 20th century. Einstein agreed to send a letter to US President Roosevelt, warning him of the danger and urging him to set up an official investigation. On 11 October 1939, Einstein's letter reached the president, who agreed to act on it. By this time, Europe was already at war.

On 9 September 1939, US President Roosevelt tells the nation that the USA will remain neutral in the war that has just broken out in Europe.

Einstein's advice

Albert Einstein's letter to Roosevelt, dated 2 August 1939, alerted the president to the possibilities of nuclear energy chain reactions – for both peaceful and military uses.

Sir,

Some recent work by E. Fermi and L. Szilard . . . leads me to expect that the element uranium may be turned into a new and important source of energy in the immediate future. Certain aspects of the situation seem to call for watchfulness and, if necessary, quick action on the part of the administration [US government]. I believe, therefore, that it is my duty to bring to your attention the following facts and recommendations.

In the course of the last four months it has been made probable . . . that it may become possible to set up nuclear energy chain reactions in a large mass of uranium, by which vast amounts of power and large quantities of new **radium**-like elements would be generated. Now it appears almost certain that this could be achieved in the immediate future.

Albert Einstein, the scientist whose theories of **matter** transformed ideas about the Universe. He later bitterly regretted his role in developing the atomic bomb.

This new phenomenon would also lead to the construction of bombs, and it is conceivable – though much less certain – that extremely powerful bombs of a new type may thus be constructed. A single bomb of this type, carried by boat or exploded in a port, might very well destroy the whole port together with some of the surrounding territory.

In view of this situation you may think it desirable to have some permanent contact maintained between the administration and the group of **physicists** working on chain reaction in America.

World war

On 1 September 1939, German armed forces had invaded Poland. Two days later, Britain and France declared war on the German aggressors. This marked the beginning of World War II. During its first phase (1939–41), **Nazi** Germany conquered most of the European continent. Britain fought on alone until June 1941, when the **Soviet Union**, invaded by Germany, became its ally.

The question of who might develop an **atomic bomb** now became more acute. Scientists in Britain solved some important problems concerning the bomb. Some of these scientists were actually Germans – they were Jews who had been driven out of their homeland by Hitler. It became clear that a rare type of **uranium** (uranium 235) was needed to build a bomb, but in smaller quantities than had been supposed. This would still cost a huge amount of money, and Britain's resources were stretched to the limit by the war effort.

In the USA, many people sympathized with Britain, and President Roosevelt provided a good deal of unofficial help. But most Americans were against becoming directly involved in the war, and the USA remained neutral.

A map of Europe showing the countries that were under German control or influence in December 1941. Only Britain and the Soviet Union were left to fight against Nazi Germany.

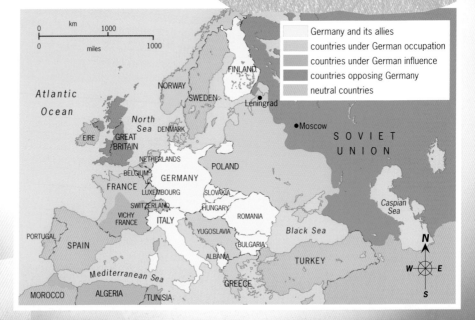

Germany and its allies
countries under German occupation
countries under German influence
countries opposing Germany
neutral countries

A chain reaction

The **physicists** Rudolf Peierls and Otto Frisch (see page 9) were refugees from Hitler's Germany who settled in Britain. Peierls described how they discovered that relatively small amounts of processed uranium might be enough to make an atomic bomb.

One day, in February or March 1940, Frisch said, 'Suppose someone gave you a quantity of pure 235 **isotope** of uranium – what would happen?' We started working out the consequences. . . We estimated the critical size to be about a pound, [500 grams] whereas speculations concerned with natural uranium had tended to come out with tons.

The invaders: German troops in armoured trucks drive through Poland in September 1939. The invasion of Poland was the event that started World War II.

That still left the question how far the chain reaction would go. . . A rough estimate . . . showed that a substantial fraction of the uranium would be split, and that therefore the energy release would be the equivalent of thousands of tons of ordinary explosive. We were quite staggered by these results: an atomic bomb was possible, after all, at least in principle!

For all we knew, the Germans could already be working on such a weapon, and the idea of Hitler getting it first was most frightening. It was our duty to inform the British government of this possibility. At the same time our conclusion had to be kept secret; if the German physicists had not yet seen the point, we did not want to draw their attention to it.

13

Pearl Harbor

The USA was deeply involved in the affairs of the Far East. At this time, most of that region was economically backward. Many countries were **colonies**, ruled by European states. But Japan was independent, industrialized and militarily strong. By the 1930s it had begun a policy of aggressive expansion, mainly targeting China. In 1931, Japan seized China's northern province of Manchuria. Then, in 1937, the Japanese began a full-scale invasion of China.

A scene of devastation after the Japanese bombing of Shanghai, China, in 1937.

When the USA could not persuade the Japanese to withdraw, President Roosevelt decided to increase the pressure by refusing to sell them oil and other materials that could be used in warfare. Since Japan had no oil of its own, its industries, and its mechanized armed forces, would soon grind to a halt. Rather than give way, the Japanese leaders decided to seize oil-rich lands in Southeast Asia. To prevent the USA from intervening, a Japanese fleet secretly crossed the Pacific and, on 7 December 1941, planes from Japanese aircraft carriers launched a devastating attack on the American fleet at Pearl Harbor, Hawaii. Within days of the attack, Germany and Italy declared war on the USA, which found itself thrown suddenly into a world war.

An infamous attack

John Garcia worked at Pearl Harbor, on the Hawaiian island of Oahu, at the time of the Japanese attack. Many years later, he told the **oral historian** Studs Terkel what it was like.

I was sixteen years old, employed as a pipe fitter apprentice at Pearl Harbor Navy Yard. On December 7, 1941, oh, around 8.00 a.m., my grandmother woke me. She informed me that the Japanese were bombing Pearl Harbor. I said, 'They're just practising.' She said, no, it was real. . . I was working on the USS *Shaw*. . . It was in flames. . . I spent the rest of the day swimming inside the harbor. . . I brought out I don't know how many bodies and how many were alive and how many dead. Another man would put them into ambulances and they'd be gone. We worked all day at that.

The following morning, I went with my tools to the [USS] *West Virginia*. It had turned turtle, totally upside down. We found a number of men inside. The *Arizona* was a total washout. Also the *Utah*. There were men in there, too. We spent about a month cutting the superstructure of the *West Virginia*, tilting it back on its hull. About 300 men we cut out of there were still alive by the eighteenth day. It took two weeks to get all the fires out. We worked around the clock for three days. There was so much excitement and confusion.

7 December 1941: US warships, stricken after the Japanese bombing of Pearl Harbor. The attack brought about the entry of the USA into World War II.

The Manhattan Project

In 1939 President Roosevelt had authorized research into the possibility of making an **atomic bomb**. But serious efforts began only in 1941, and were further speeded up by the USA's entry into the war. The quest was code-named the Manhattan Project.

At first, research was carried out in Chicago where, in December 1942, the Italian **physicist** Enrico Fermi built the world's first 'atomic pile' – a **nuclear reactor** in which a controlled chain reaction was successfully created. Soon afterwards, the Manhattan Project moved to Los Alamos in the desert country of **New Mexico**. This remote location made it easier to keep the work secret. Hundreds of scientists were assembled at Los Alamos, under the leadership of an American physicist, J. Robert Oppenheimer.

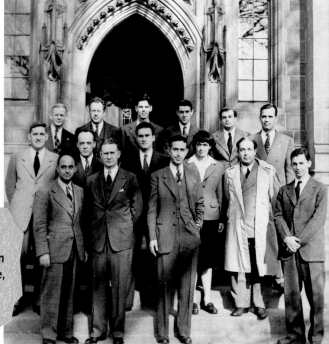

A gathering of scientists at the University of Chicago in 1946. All were involved in creating an 'atomic pile'; the leading figure, Enrico Fermi, stands at the far left of the front row.

An army officer, General Leslie R. Groves, commanded the entire project, maintaining an extraordinary level of security to keep it a secret. There were still immense technical and practical problems to overcome. Tens of thousands of workers were employed at other sites in manufacturing the necessary materials, and billions of dollars were spent. Finally, after three years, 'the Bomb' appeared to be ready.

Atomic city

General Groves, who was in overall charge of the Manhattan Project, described Oak Ridge, Tennessee. This was a secret engineering works, making everything needed by the scientists based at Los Alamos. Oak Ridge became, in effect, a town. It was not the only large-scale industrial development in this extraordinary project.

The installation occupied a rectangular-shaped Government Reservation, 93 square miles in area. . . A maximum employment of 82,000 was reached in May, 1945.

In the course of our work, Oak Ridge grew to be Tennessee's fifth city by population... The area's motor transportation system was the largest in the Southeastern United States. Because it was a closed military area, we had to provide all the normal community, municipal and other government services.

The first phase of our planning program called for the construction of more than three thousand family quarters, several apartment buildings and dormitories and numerous trailer parks, along with all the community facilities. The second and third phases were carried out along similar lines, but on a far greater scale.

The school system was based on a policy that the community should be provided with educational standards of high quality.

We also had to provide for the recreation and welfare of the inhabitants of Oak Ridge... We provided motion picture theatres, soda fountains, snack bars, athletic fields and even a weekly newspaper... Eventually, Oak Ridge possessed every service that might be found in any typical American community.

Testing the bomb

By July 1945, the Los Alamos scientists believed they could make a bomb based on producing a chain reaction. This could be done by using **uranium**, or a newly created element (basic substance), **plutonium**. Now a full-scale test was needed. The site chosen was the Alamogordo US Army Air Base in the **New Mexico** desert. The test was code-named 'Trinity'.

The bomb, nicknamed Fat Man, was filled with a plutonium core surrounded with explosives; detonating them would set off a chain reaction in the plutonium. Fat Man was not dropped, but was lodged at the top of a 30-metre-high steel tower.

The detonation took place on 16 July at 5.30 a.m., some time before sunrise. The closest observers were in a concrete bunker about 10 kilometres (6 miles) away. They were wearing sunglasses, but were still nearly blinded by the flash that lit up the night sky. Then came a blast of heat, a shock wave, a terrible roar, and a fireball followed by a soaring mushroom cloud. Almost everyone was delighted that years of work had been rewarded, though they were also awed by what they had witnessed. Oppenheimer said, quoting an ancient Indian Hindu text, 'Now I am become Death, the shatterer of worlds.'

After testing the bomb. In the centre of the photo, J. Robert Oppenheimer (in white hat) and General Groves (in uniform) examine the area directly below the explosion. Its intense heat melted the steel tower and turned the desert sand into glass.

A searing light

One of those who witnessed the test from a concrete bunker was Brigadier General Thomas F. Farrell. He described it in a long report.

Dr Oppenheimer. . . grew tenser as the last seconds ticked off. He scarcely breathed. He held on to a post to steady himself. For the last few seconds, he stared directly ahead and then when the announcer shouted 'Now!' and there came this tremendous burst of light followed shortly thereafter by the deep growling roar of the explosion, his face relaxed into an expression of tremendous relief. Several of the observers standing [at the] back of the shelter to watch the lighting effects were knocked flat by the blast.

The tension in the room let up and all started congratulating each other. Everyone sensed, 'This is it!'. . . No man-made phenomenon of such tremendous power had ever occurred before. The lighting effects beggared description. The whole country was lighted by a searing light with the intensity many times that of the midday sun. It was golden, purple, violet, gray and blue. It lighted every peak, crevasse and ridge of the nearby mountain range with a clarity and beauty that cannot be described... Thirty seconds after the explosion came, first, the air blast pressing hard against the people and things, to be followed almost immediately by the strong, sustained, awesome roar which warned of doomsday. . . It had to be witnessed to be realized.

Leaders in conference

The Alamogordo test took place too late to influence the war in Europe. By May 1945 Germany and Italy had surrendered. It turned out that Germany had not progressed very far with its atomic research, put off by the enormous expense.

The war against Japan was not yet over, but its defeat seemed certain. The Japanese navy and airforce had largely been destroyed. US raids, by as many as 300 bombers at a time, were burning down Japan's cities with **incendiary bombs**. As the US military knew, most Japanese buildings were made of wood, so these 'fire bombs' were incredibly destructive, killing many more Japanese than the **atomic bombs** would later do. **Allied** armies were now poised to invade Japan itself. Some Japanese leaders realized that defeat was inevitable, but the military commanders who dominated the government would not consider the unconditional surrender demanded by the **Allies**.

In July 1945 the US president, Harry S Truman, went to a conference at Potsdam in Germany with Britain's Winston Churchill and the Soviet leader, Joseph Stalin. The Allied leaders wanted to arrange the affairs of post-war Europe and discuss the situation in the Far East. Although Truman distrusted the Soviets, he wanted Russia to enter the war against Japan, and Stalin agreed. Then, while he was still at the conference, Truman was told of the successful bomb test.

American B-29 aircraft drop incendiary bombs on Yokohama, Japan, in May 1945. The biggest US missions involved hundreds of bombers dropping thousands of bombs.

A changed man

Henry Stimson was the US secretary [minister] for war. His diary shows how the news of the successful atom bomb test affected Truman's behaviour.

The Allied leaders, Churchill, Truman and Stalin, at the Potsdam Conference, where Truman learned that the atomic bomb test had been a success.

At ten-forty. . . I again went to the British headquarters and talked to the Prime Minister [Churchill] and Lord Cherwell [Churchill's scientific adviser] for over an hour. Churchill read Groves' report [on the Alamogordo test] in full. He told me that he had noticed at the meeting of the Three [Truman, Churchill and Stalin] yesterday that Truman was evidently much fortified by something that had happened and that he stood up to the Russians in a most emphatic and decisive manner, telling them as to certain demands that they absolutely could not have them and that the United States was entirely against them. He [Churchill] said 'Now I know what happened to Truman yesterday. I couldn't understand it. When he got to the meeting after having read this report he was a changed man. He told the Russians just where they got on and off and generally bossed the whole meeting'. Churchill said he now understood how this pepping up had taken place and that he felt the same way.

Making the decision

On 25 July 1945, President Truman authorized the use of **atomic bombs** against Japan. The USA and Britain issued a statement, the Potsdam Declaration, which gave the Japanese a last chance to surrender. But the declaration did not mention that the USA possessed a super-weapon, nor did it deal with the main Japanese objection to an unconditional surrender. The Japanese feared the USA might remove, or even execute, their emperor, Hirohito. Originally the Potsdam Declaration had contained a promise that the emperor could remain, but Truman finally decided to remove it.

Dropping the bomb meant that tens of thousands of civilians would die. But during the war, all sides had become used to the bombing of civilian targets. And American hatred of the Japanese was very strong. The Japanese had attacked Pearl Harbor, without warning, during peacetime. They had massacred and raped many thousands of Chinese people. And they treated **Allied** prisoners of war with monstrous inhumanity, murdering and torturing them or working them to death on projects like the notorious Burma-Thailand Railway. Understandably, wartime propaganda portrayed them as devilishly cruel while showing American fire-bombing of Japanese cities as heroic. Such facts certainly influenced the decision that President Truman had to make.

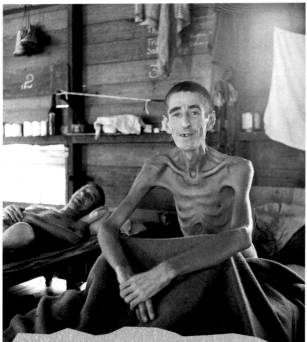

A British serviceman after several years as a Japanese prisoner of war. The USA and Britain were outraged and horrified by the brutal treatment of such prisoners by the Japanese.

The most terrible thing

On 25 July 1945, President Truman gave the order to use the atomic bomb. This is an extract from his diary for that day. His way of writing suggests that he was uneasy about his decision.

We have discovered the most terrible bomb in the history of the world . . . we think we have found the way to cause a disintegration of the atom. An experiment in the **New Mexican** desert was startling – to put it mildly. . . This weapon is to be used against Japan between now and August 10. I have told the secretary of war, Mr Stimson, to use it so that military objectives and soldiers are the target and not women and children. Even if the Japs are savages, ruthless, merciless and fanatic, we as the leader of the world for the common welfare cannot drop this terrible bomb on the old capital or the new. He and I are in accord [agreement]. The target will be a purely military one and we will issue a warning statement asking the Japs to surrender and save lives. I'm sure they will not do that, but we will have given them the chance. It is certainly a good thing for the world that Hitler's crowd or Stalin's did not discover this atomic bomb. It seems to be the most terrible thing ever discovered, but it can be made the most useful.

Not so little: the atomic bomb, nicknamed Little Boy, that was dropped on Hiroshima on 6 August 1945.

Mixed motives

Even in the heat of war, there were some scientists and military leaders who disagreed with Truman's decision to use the **atomic bomb** against Japan. But it was only later, when hatreds had become less intense, that the decision became really controversial. Among historians, it still is. The main justification advanced for dropping it has usually been that by shortening the war it saved lives – even, in the long run, Japanese lives.

Battle after battle had shown that the Japanese would fight almost to the last man rather than surrender. Their casualties were frightful, but many Americans died too. The Japanese also recruited **kamikazes** – young men who flew suicide missions, crashing their planes into US ships. Thanks to the atomic bomb, the USA and Britain did not have to invade Japan. Some authorities claimed that the dropping of the bomb was justified because an invasion would have cost the USA half a million casualties – though others disagreed and put the figure as low as 40,000.

Other motives have been suggested for using the bomb. A spectacular success would justify its enormous cost. It would end the war before the Russians came in to share the spoils, such as claiming a role in the post-war government of Japan. And it would warn Stalin not to cross swords with the USA. Several of these motives may have been present at the same time. Which of them was the most important is still being argued about.

A Japanese kamikaze plane, on a mission to crash into a US warship. This one has been shot down before reaching its target.

Argument at the dinner table

General Dwight D. Eisenhower was the **Allied** supreme commander during the war in Europe, and later became president of the USA. In 1963 he recalled having dinner with Henry Stimson at the time of the Potsdam Conference.

Little Boy is winched into the bomb-bay aboard the plane chosen to attack Hiroshima.

Stimson got this cable saying the bomb had been perfected and was ready to be dropped. . . Well, I listened and I didn't volunteer anything [comment on it] because, after all, my war was over in Europe and it wasn't up to me. But I was getting more and more depressed just thinking about it. Then he asked for my opinion, so I told him I was against it on two counts. First, the Japanese were ready to surrender and it wasn't necessary to hit them with that awful thing. Second, I hated to see our country be the first to use such a weapon. Well . . . the old gentleman got furious. And I can see how he would. After all, it had been his responsibility to push for all the huge expenditure to develop the bomb, which of course he had a right to do and was right to do. Still, it was an awful problem.

Flight over Japan

The Americans had already drawn up a list of possible targets. They were Japanese cities that had not yet been under serious attack. That way, the devastating effect of the bomb would be clear. Kyoto and Hiroshima headed the list. But since Kyoto was an ancient city, Hiroshima, an industrial city with a population of 300,000, was chosen.

The mission was carried out by a specially formed bomber group which had been training for months on the Pacific island of Tinian. A **uranium**-based bomb, nicknamed Little Boy, was loaded on to a B-29 bomber, the *Enola Gay*. The aircraft was named after the mother of the group's commander, Colonel Paul Tibbets, who flew the plane to Hiroshima. He was the only man on board who knew exactly what the aircraft was carrying, although the crew realized it must be something special.

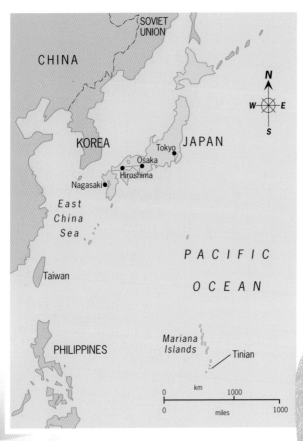

Enola Gay took off at 2.45 a.m. on 6 August 1945. By 8.15 a.m. the citizens of Hiroshima were going about their daily lives. The *Enola Gay* dropped Little Boy by parachute, and two of the three detonator switches were activated. At 8.16 a.m., when the bomb was 580 metres above the ground, a radar signal from the *Enola Gay* activated the final switch and detonated it.

A map of Japan showing, far to the south, the Pacific island of Tinian, from which the *Enola Gay* was sent on its mission.

The mushroom cloud

Sergeant George Caron, the *Enola Gay's* tail gunner, recorded what he could see as the plane circled Hiroshima after dropping the bomb.

The B-29 bomber *Enola Gay*, which dropped an **atomic bomb** on Hiroshima. In front stand the ground crew, with the pilot, Colonel Tibbets, in the centre.

A column of smoke rising fast. It has a fiery red core. A bubbling mass, purple-gray in colour, with that red core. It's all turbulent. Fires are springing up everywhere, like flames shooting out of a huge bed of coals. I am starting to count the fires. One, two, three, four, five, six . . . fourteen, fifteen . . . it's impossible. There are too many to count. Here it comes, the mushroom shape... It's coming this way. It's like a mass of bubbling molasses. The mushroom is spreading out. It's maybe a mile or two wide and half a mile high. It's growing up and up and up. It's nearly level with us and climbing. It's very black, but there is a purplish tint to the cloud. The base of the mushroom . . . is shot through with flames. The city must be below that. The flames and smoke are billowing out, whirling out into the foothills. The hills are disappearing under the smoke. All I can see now of the city is the main dock and what looks like an airfield.

Blinding flash, burning wind

Little Boy was aimed at the Aioi Bridge in the centre of Hiroshima. It was 250 metres off target, and Ground Zero (the area immediately beneath the bomb) was a hospital. Moments after the explosion, all that remained of the hospital were a few concrete uprights. For individuals anywhere near it, the explosion was like a silent 'sunburst' of light and heat, lasting less than a second.

Thousands of people within 500 metres or so of the blast were killed instantly. They vanished, or became standing corpses composed of ash that crumbled at a touch. If any nearby walls remained standing, the victims' shadows were burned into them. The flash was followed by a searing heatwave. People as far as 3.5 kilometres (2 miles) away were severely burned. Their clothes were welded to their bodies or burst into flames. In many cases, flesh simply melted or internal organs were boiled away.

Then came the shock wave. Houses were flattened and, 20 kilometres (12.4 miles) away, the *Enola Gay* was rocked so hard that Tibbets thought anti-aircraft guns had opened fire. The blast caught up masses of rubble, dust and broken glass, which stripped away clothing and tore flesh. And then firestorms raced through the city and people jumped into the river to escape. Everywhere, clocks and watches stopped at 8.16 a.m.

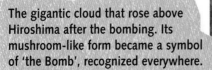

The gigantic cloud that rose above Hiroshima after the bombing. Its mushroom-like form became a symbol of 'the Bomb', recognized everywhere.

City in ruins

Sumiko Kirihara, a fourteen-year-old student, was lucky
to survive when the bomb was dropped on Hiroshima.

Our family decided to hold a reunion on August 6 and to
take a commemorative photograph of all of us together...
The photographer was supposed to arrive at eight in the
morning but was late for some reason. Consequently, we
did not go into the garden, but stayed indoors... Suddenly
a tremendous cracking sound nearly split my eardrums.
A pale blue flash temporarily blinded me; then total
darkness enveloped
everything. When
the light once
again penetrated
the blackness,
I saw the city
of Hiroshima
reduced to ruins.

A sinister memento
of the bombing of
Hiroshima: one of
many watches and
clocks from the city
in which the hands
stopped for ever at
the time of the
detonation, 8.16 a.m.

Fire now raged
everywhere. A
black rain fell
[because of polluted air], and dun
[brown] smoke hid the sun. As we
made our way to the Kyobashi
River, whirlwinds tossed sheets
of scorched galvanized iron along
the streets. Then the winds struck the
river, sending columns of water upwards, dashing boats
about. . . In terror, I dug a hole in the sand, crawled into
it. . . One whirlwind followed another, raising clouds of
sand that lashed at my back like countless needles.
Unable to bear the winds any longer, we climbed to a
piece of open land by the river. . . We spent the night by
the river.

Scenes of horror

The ordeal went on. Charred corpses and dying people lay everywhere. Survivors shambled or crawled about, many of them dazed, naked and horribly injured. Scorched, thirsty people flung themselves into rivers and streams. Their numbers increased as firestorms raged through the city, and many were drowned in the confusion. Others, trapped beneath rubble or too badly injured to move, were burned to death.

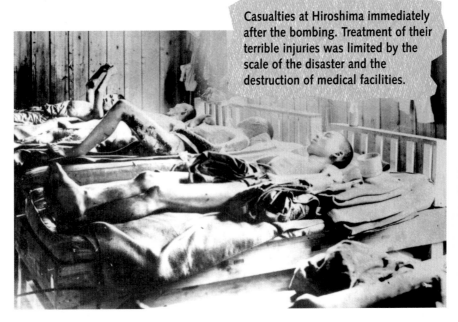

Casualties at Hiroshima immediately after the bombing. Treatment of their terrible injuries was limited by the scale of the disaster and the destruction of medical facilities.

Meanwhile an enormous mushroom cloud, thickened with smoke and ash, blotted out the light. American observer aircraft flew over the city all day, but could see little through the dust and floating debris. Beneath them lay a blackened and burning area extending some 10.5 square kilometres (4 square miles).

As the mushroom cloud cooled, showers of greasy black rain fell, staining everything it touched. Until help arrived from outside, people had to fend for themselves. Most medical centres, and most of the city's medical staff and supplies, had perished. When emergency treatment stations were set up, overworked doctors had to be ruthless, treating only people who had a reasonable chance of recovering from their injuries.

Vision of hell

Satoko Matsumoto, a widow, and her two-year-old daughter, were inside 'when a tremendous flash of light suddenly swept over everything'.

Suddenly . . . the house collapsed, pinning us under the wreckage. . . Slowly and carefully, I crawled out. . . Once out of doors, I was appalled at what I saw. Every building in the city seemed to have been razed.

In the swirling dust and smoke, I could make out ghostly human figures moving towards us from the east. . . At first, I thought I noticed tatters of clothing hanging from some of them. Then I realized that it was skin flayed from their bodies to expose raw flesh.

Fire had started spreading from all directions . . . I heard someone shout that we must hurry if we wanted to cross the river... A man who had been walking in front of me fell to the ground. Putting out my hand to help him, I saw that he was already dead. One after another, people died, some of them with a cry for water on their lips.

Then it began to rain, large, heavy drops lashing the wounded flesh of the burned. . . It was not clear and fresh, but dark, turbid, and sticky, like crude oil. It adhered to my hair and to my skin, which were already covered with reddish dust from the debris of my collapsed house.

The destroyed city: an aerial view of Hiroshima, its city centre a burned-out wasteland.

Heroes' welcome

The *Enola Gay* circled Hiroshima three times before leaving. While it was circling, tail gunner Caron took photographs. Tibbets ordered radar officer Jacob Besser to tape-record the crew's reactions, including Caron's eyewitness description (see page 27). A typical comment was Besser's: 'It's pretty terrific. What a relief it works.' The co-pilot, Robert A. Lewis, was writing his own unofficial 'log' of the operation. He is said to have shared the general enthusiasm, though later he scribbled: 'My God, what have we done?'

Radio messages to Tinian announced the success of the mission. The *Enola Gay* touched down at North Field, Tinian, at 2.58 p.m., having flown more than 3100 kilometres (1926 miles) in just over twelve hours. When the crew emerged from the hatch of the aircraft, they were met by senior officers, thousands of servicemen, and reporters and cameramen. Tibbets was decorated on the spot with the Distinguished Service Cross. The crew were **debriefed** and the servicemen celebrated with a big party. The rest of the world remained unaware that the war had taken a new and decisive turn.

The *Enola Gay* comes in to land on Tinian island after completing its mission. It received a wildly enthusiastic reception, and Colonel Tibbets, the leader of the operation, was decorated.

A news report

The day before the bombing, the London *Observer* newspaper carried an assessment of the war situation: Japan would probably surrender – within a few months. This shows that the dropping of the bomb was a complete surprise, and one that would transform the situation.

Observer

5 August 1945

Early Collapse of Japan Predicted Fleets Mass for Invasion

from Gordon Walker,
British Pacific Fleet HQ

The collapse or surrender of Japan within the next few months was viewed here today by British Fleet authorities as a very definite possibility. At the same time these officials, together with high [US] military leaders in Guam and Manila, are proceeding on the assumption that the only way Japan can be defeated is by further whittling down of her military strength and then invading the home islands.

High military authorities with whom I have recently talked at Guam are predicting that the war might be over by September this year. This is the result of analyses of information which reveals Japan's rapidly declining military position.

Strikes by the Combined Fleet, which is still, presumably, somewhere off Japan this weekend . . . are an integral part of the preliminary phase leading to invasion. They were timed to be part of a sudden spurt in **Allied** propaganda pressure.

The destroyed city

At Hiroshima, the suffering and devastation were on an awesome scale. There were probably about 260,000 civilians and 40,000 soldiers in Hiroshima. Around 80,000 people are believed to have been killed at 8.16 a.m. They included many schoolgirls, who were being employed to make firebreaks, and American prisoners of war held in Hiroshima Castle.

Tens of thousands more perished in the next few weeks. Some expired quickly from their injuries, but others, apparently unharmed, suddenly became ill and died. The reasons for this 'bomb sickness' (as people in Hiroshima called it) were only understood later (see page 42). As the process continued over the years, the death toll may have risen to more than 200,000.

Meanwhile, huge numbers of people were made homeless by the destruction of around 60,000 buildings. Many survivors tried to flee, finding little help in nearby villages that were already overcrowded and short of food. Local relief was slow to arrive, having to force its way down rivers choked with bodies. There were no power supplies and roads were impassable. In Tokyo, the Japanese capital, some 350 kilometres (217 miles) away, it was at first assumed that the bombing was just another heavy air raid. Even when the government realized what had happened, it was able to do little.

Hiroshima, September 1946: a year after the bombing, the city is still in ruins. A gutted building stands next to an even more thoroughly destroyed structure, reduced to a mass of twisted steel girders.

City of the dead

Marcel Junod, director-general of the Red Cross, visited
Hiroshima a month after the bombing, on 9 September 1945.
A Japanese journalist acted as his guide.

The Japanese broke off and then pronounced one word with
indescribable but restrained emotion: 'Look.'

We were then rather less than four miles away from the Aioi
Bridge . . . but already the roofs of the houses around us had
lost their tiles and the grass was yellow along the roadside.
At three miles from the centre. . . the houses were already
destroyed, their roofs had fallen in and the beams jutted out
from the wreckage of their walls. But so far it was only the
usual spectacle presented by towns damaged by ordinary
high explosives.

About two and a half miles from the centre of the town all the
buildings had been burnt out and destroyed. Only traces of the
foundations and piles of debris and rusty charred ironwork
were left. This zone was like the devastated areas of Tokyo,
Osaka and Kobé after the mass fall of **incendiaries**.

At three-quarters of a mile . . . nothing at all was left.
Everything had disappeared. It was a stony waste littered with
debris and twisted girders. The incandescent breath of the fire
had swept away every obstacle.

We got out of the car and made our way slowly through the
ruins into the centre of the dead city. Absolute silence reigned
in the whole necropolis [city of the dead].

The news breaks

On 6 August, the USA and Britain issued public statements. President Truman's was jubilant: 'We spent $200,000,000,000 on the greatest scientific gamble in history – and won.' The USA told the Japanese that, unless they surrendered, they would face 'ruin from the air the like of which has never been seen on this earth'. The British statement, drafted by Winston Churchill, paid tribute to American genius, but showed an awareness that 'the bomb' was a fearful gift to humanity.

The official Japanese reaction was delayed until 8 August. It said that dropping the **atomic bomb** would 'brand the enemy for ages to come as the destroyer of mankind'. Radio Tokyo gave a brief but accurate account, describing a city where 'practically all living things . . . were literally seared to death.' However, Japan did not surrender.

Meanwhile, at Los Alamos, most of the scientists were overjoyed, though a minority had opposed the use of the bomb. The secret had been kept so well that most Americans were astonished as well as delighted. And young servicemen, realizing the war was effectively over, were hugely relieved.

The destruction of Hiroshima, reported in a US newspaper published at Santa Fé, the nearest town to Los Alamos.

We were going to live...
Paul Fussell, now a well-known American writer, was serving in the US army in August 1945. Although he had been seriously wounded not long before, he knew he would be taking part in the planned invasion of Japan.

I was a 21-year-old second lieutenant leading a rifle platoon. . . When the bombs dropped [on Hiroshima and Nagasaki] and news began to circulate that the invasion of Japan would not, after all, take place, that we would not be obliged to run up the beaches near Tokyo assault-firing while being mortared and shelled . . . we cried with relief and joy. We were going to live. We were going to grow up to adulthood after all.

A sense of unease
The refugee scientist Otto Frisch was now working at Los Alamos. His reaction to the news was very different from Fussell's.

Some three weeks after Alamogordo, there was a sudden noise in the laboratory, of running footsteps and yelling voices. Somebody opened my door and shouted 'Hiroshima has been destroyed!'; about a hundred thousand people were thought to have been killed. I still remember the feeling of unease, indeed nausea, when I saw how many of my friends were rushing to the telephone to book tables at the La Fonda hotel in Santa Fé, in order to celebrate.

Second strike

Though urged to surrender, the Japanese were given very little time to make up their minds. Later, this US policy decision was strongly criticized. On 9 August, a second mission was flown. A B-29, named *Bock's Car* and piloted by Major Charles Sweeney, left Tinian at 2.56 a.m. It was carrying Fat Man, a **plutonium** bomb like the one used at the Alamogordo test.

The weather was uncertain and the mission suffered delays. When Sweeney reached the target, the city of Kokura, it was hidden by smoke and mist. So *Bock's Car* went on to the second target on the list: Nagasaki.

By this time, there was only enough fuel for a single bombing run. Nagasaki was covered by thick clouds, but the bombardier spotted a gap and at 11.02 a.m. Fat Man was released through it. Although it was dropped 2.5 kilometres off target, the effect was still devastating. Unlike Hiroshima, Nagasaki was hilly, and that contained the blast to some extent. Even so, 40,000 people were killed within a short time, and later the total number of dead reached 77,000.

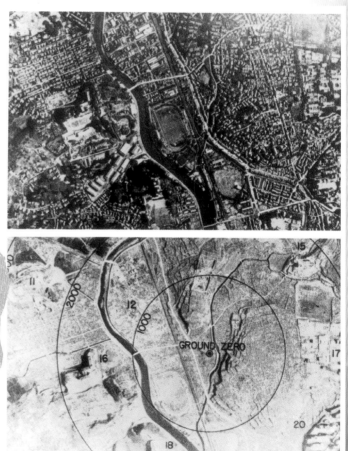

Nagasaki, before and after. Aerial photographs from the US Strategic Bombing Survey show the impact on the city of the bomb dropped on 9 August 1945.

Nagasaki

Bill Laurence was a science journalist attached to the Manhattan Project. He travelled in the observer plane that accompanied *Bock's Car*, and wrote about the strange beauty of the mushroom cloud.

Observers in the tail of our ship saw a giant ball of fire rise as though from the bowels of the earth, belching forth enormous smoke rings. Next they saw a giant pillar of purple fire 10,000 feet high, [3000 metres] shooting skyward with enormous speed. . . Awestruck we watched the pillar of fire shoot upwards . . . becoming ever more alive as it climbed skyward through the white clouds.

Terrified citizens flee the plutonium bomb attack on Nagasaki.

Just when it appeared as though the whole thing had settled down . . . there came shooting out of the top a giant mushroom that increased the height of the pillar to 45,000 feet [14,000 metres]. The mushroom top was even more alive than the pillar, seething and boiling in a white fury of creamy foam, sizzling upwards and then descending earthwards.

In a few seconds it had freed itself from its gigantic stem and floated upwards with a tremendous speed, its momentum carrying it into the stratosphere to a height of 60,000 feet [18,300 metres]. But no sooner did this happen than another mushroom smaller in size than the first one began emerging out of the pillar. It was as though a decapitated monster was growing a new head.

As the first mushroom floated off into the blue it changed its shape into a flowerlike form, its giant petals curving downward, creamy white outside, rose-coloured inside. It still retained that shape when we last gazed at it from a distance of about 200 miles [320 kilometres].

Japan surrenders

By early 1945, many Japanese political leaders realized that the war was lost. But they were civilians, unwilling to challenge the military leaders – who had been known to assassinate those who opposed them. Surrender was hard to face for the Japanese, who had never been conquered and had been trained to believe that honour required a fight to the death. And the **Allies**' demand for unconditional surrender made things harder still. The possibility that the Allies intended to remove their emperor gave the military an excuse to go on fighting.

With nothing decided, Japan was struck by two new blows on 9 August: the USA bombed Nagasaki, and the **Soviet Union** declared war and began to overwhelm Japanese forces in Manchuria. That evening, Japan's Supreme War Council was still evenly divided. Then the prime minister asked Emperor Hirohito to decide the matter. This was an unprecedented move. The Japanese emperor was revered as a god-like figure, but he was not normally involved in making political decisions. Now he told Japan's leaders that they must 'bear the unbearable' and surrender. Japan accepted the Allies' terms on 14 August, and on 2 September the formal surrender was signed on board the US battleship *Missouri*.

The emperor speaks

When the Japanese Supreme War Council met after Nagasaki, it could not agree whether to surrender or fight on. The Japanese emperor, Hirohito, normally left political decisions to others, but this time he spoke.

I have given serious thought to the situation prevailing at home and abroad and have concluded that continuing the war can only mean destruction for the nation and a prolongation of bloodshed and cruelty in the world. . . I cannot bear to see my innocent people struggle any longer. Ending the war is the only way to restore world peace and to relieve the nation from the terrible distress with which it is burdened.

I cannot help feeling sad when I think of the people who have served me so faithfully, the soldiers and sailors who have been killed or wounded in far off battles, the families who have lost all their worldly goods, and often their lives, in the air raids at home. It goes without saying that it is unbearable for me to see the brave and loyal fighting men of Japan disarmed. It is equally unbearable that others who have rendered me devoted service should now be punished as instigators of war. Nevertheless, the time has come when we must bear the unbearable.

I . . . swallow my tears and sanction the proposal to accept the **Allied** proclamation on the basis outlined by the Foreign Minister.

Japan's official surrender takes place on 2 September 1945. The photograph captures the moment, on board the USS *Missouri*, when the Chief of the Japanese Army General Staff signed the document.

Invisible rays

Within a day or two of the atomic explosions, sickness began to afflict individuals who appeared to have escaped without serious harm. Some began to vomit and died quickly. Others were affected much later, suddenly becoming utterly exhausted. People found that cuts and scratches caused by the explosion would not heal, or kept breaking open. Many were even more severely affected. Their hair began to fall out, their gums bled, a purplish rash appeared on their skin, and they suffered from severe diarrhoea.

The unimaginable heat of the atomic explosion has burned the pattern on this Japanese victim's kimono into her skin.

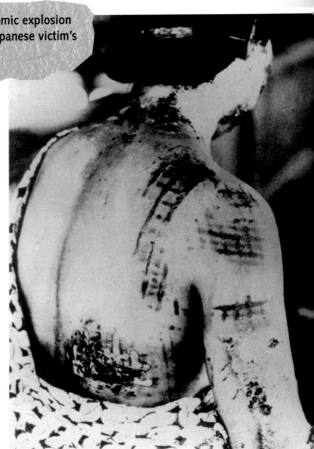

These were the results of radiation – rays given off by the explosion, including X-rays, **gamma rays** and **neutrons.** The radiation affected people who returned to the bombed cities, and it was also dispersed in the form of fall-out – airborne nuclear debris. Among the effects of different forms of radiation were the destruction of bone marrow, making it impossible to resist infections, and cell changes leading to cancer and leukaemia. Most of the women who had been pregnant at the time of the Hiroshima and Nagasaki bombings had miscarriages. Many children were born with disabilities, but others developed radiation-related illnesses years later.

The horror of my life…

Mihoko Takeuchi was not born when Hiroshima was bombed, but she still suffered from its effects.

I never saw the horrors of the war . . . because I was not born until October 2, 1945. . . But in October 1958, while I was a first-year student, I noticed red spots on my arms . . . glancing in the mirror, I saw that my gums were coated with dark, coagulated blood. . . Terrified by something that I could not understand, I felt as if I were falling into a bottomless pit.

My mother explained that at the time of the Hiroshima bombing, when eight months pregnant with me, she had been at a place only four kilometres [2.5 miles] from the hypocentre. [She was cured, but] one day in 1962, when I was a second-year student in a girls' high school, I discovered a red spot on my knee. Stunned, I . . . found many more such spots. As had happened years earlier, my gums were coated with coagulated blood.

I was released from the hospital, but not from the horror of my life. From time to time, my condition became so unbearable that I wanted to kill myself.

Some time later, I . . . resolved not to give in to my sickness. I did not give in and am now living a fulfilled life, though I am still not in perfect health.

Occupied Japan

At the end of August 1945, Japan was occupied by American forces. As supreme commander, General Douglas MacArthur became effectively the ruler of Japan. Some Japanese leaders were tried and hanged for war crimes.

Despite their commitment to promoting **democracy** in Japan, the US authorities refused to permit references to the **atomic bombings** in Japanese newspapers. They also denied that the bombings would produce long-lasting radiation effects, although scientists at Los Alamos had recognized that these were likely to occur. However, in 1945 an Australian journalist, Wilfred Burchett, alerted the world by describing, in the British *Daily Express* newspaper, what he had seen at Hiroshima ('people are still dying, mysteriously and horribly'). However, in most respects US rule in Japan was remarkably fair and generous. Civilian democracy was promoted and the country was rebuilt. And with American help the economy was put on such a firm basis that in time Japan became one of the world's leading industrial countries.

Even after the war, American unease about the bombings continued. In 1951 a peace treaty gave Japan back its independence, but Japan had to agree not to press for compensation for bomb victims. The Japanese government was equally anxious to forget the past. During this period the victims (known in Japan as *hibakusha*, 'explosion-affected persons') were mainly dependent on help from the Red Cross and other charities. It was only in 1957 that the Japanese government provided the *hibakusha* with allowances and free medical treatment.

General Douglas MacArthur, US governor of Japan, with the Japanese emperor, Hirohito. No longer regarded as a god, the emperor remained the symbolic head of a new, democratic Japan.

Disputed evidence

When the Australian journalist Wilfred Burchett revealed evidence of radiation sickness at Hiroshima, the USA continued to deny it. Burchett describes his experience at a press conference that was held to try to discredit him.

The conference was nearing its end, but it was clear that the main purpose was to deny my dispatch from Hiroshima, which the *Daily Express* had made available to the world press, that people were dying from after effects of the bomb. A scientist in brigadier general's uniform explained that there could be no question of atomic radiation – which could cause the symptoms I had described – because the bombs had been exploded at such a height as to obviate any risk of 'residual radiation'.

My first question was whether the briefing officer had been to Hiroshima. He had not . . . I described what I had seen – and asked for explanations. It was very gentlemanly at first, a scientist explaining things to a layman. . . Eventually the exchanges narrowed down to my asking how he explained the fish still dying when they entered a stream running through the centre of the city. . . 'I was taken to a spot in the city outskirts and watched live fish turning their white stomachs upwards as they entered a certain stretch of the river. After that they were dead within seconds.'

The spokesman looked pained. 'I'm afraid you've fallen victim to Japanese propaganda', he said, and sat down.

Balance of fear

Soon after the end of World War II, the victorious **Allies** fell out.
Most of the world became divided between 'the West' (including
the USA and Western Europe) and the Communist bloc (the **Soviet
Union** and its allies). The conflict was known as the **Cold War**,
because it involved an icy hostility rather than a 'hot' shooting war.
But all-out war seldom seemed far away, and both sides armed
feverishly. In the atmosphere of the Cold War, people who opposed
the idea of making more and more nuclear weapons became
unpopular. This happened to J. Robert Oppenheimer, the scientist
who had led the Manhattan Project. He was considered a security risk
and was no longer allowed access to military secrets. Other scientists
also came to regret their work at Los Alamos, as nuclear weapons
spread from country to country across the world.

Atomic bombs were acquired by the Soviet Union, Britain, France
and China. Constant testing poisoned Bikini Atoll in the Pacific and
other sites. Soon atomic bombs were replaced by immensely more
powerful **hydrogen bombs**, by rockets that could carry nuclear
weapons across continents (**ICBMs**), and by **neutron bombs**.
Eventually the two sides had enough weaponry to destroy civilization
and perhaps all human life. During episodes such as the 1962 **Cuban
Missile Crisis**, the end of the world seemed very close.

US President Kennedy (centre front) and military
leaders during the 1962 Cuban Missile Crisis,
when a nuclear war between the USA and the
Soviet Union seemed close.

On the brink of extinction

Former US Defence Secretary Robert McNamara recalled the Cuban Missile Crisis, when a nuclear war between the USA and the Soviet Union seemed a real possibility.

On Friday evening, October 26, we received the most extraordinary diplomatic message I have ever seen... It was a long, rambling message signed by [the Soviet leader] Khrushchev. The text had obviously been dictated by a man under intense emotional pressure. Khrushchev said... 'If war should break out, it would not be in our power to stop it - war ends when it has rolled through cities and villages, everywhere sowing death and destruction.'

Tensions continued to rise that Saturday ... we chose to reply to Khrushchev's ... communication, emphasizing that we had no intention of invading Cuba if the Soviet offensive forces were removed ... But we made clear that if they were not removed, further action by the United States would follow.

I will not speculate on what that further action might have been, but I do know that as I left the White House and walked through the garden to my car to return to the Pentagon on that beautiful fall [autumn] evening, I feared I might never live to see another Saturday night.

Hazards of the nuclear age

News about the effects of the **atomic bomb** gradually spread through articles such as Wilfred Burchett's and the American writer John Hersey's famous book *Hiroshima*, published in 1952. Evidence about fallout also accumulated. In 1954, Japanese fishermen aboard their boat, the *Lucky Dragon*, were enveloped in radioactive ash from a bomb test on Bikini Atoll. All of them became sick, and one died.

March 1954: on a Japanese fishing boat, working in a supposedly safe area, both men and fish suffered from the fallout after a US hydrogen bomb test at Bikini Atoll. Here, Japanese scientists use a **Geiger counter** to check the fish.

Fear for the world's future spurred some people to action. **Physicists** such as Szilard, Oppenheimer and Fermi tried to persuade the US government, and later other nations, not to make the **hydrogen bomb**. Movements in favour of peace and disarmament sprang up, including Britain's Campaign for Nuclear Disarmament (CND), founded in 1958.

None of this seemed to have much influence on the behaviour of governments. The arms race continued, principally between the two 'superpowers', the USA and the **Soviet Union**. Eventually, in the 1970s, the superpowers did make some agreements to limit their nuclear arsenals, although these remained huge. Meanwhile, nuclear energy was also used in many countries for peaceful industrial purposes, though accidents at Harrisburg (USA) and, much more seriously, Chernobyl (in the Ukraine) showed that this also involved risks.

A danger to mankind

On 30 October 1949, the General Advisory Committee to the US Atomic Energy Commission opposed the development of a 'superweapon' (the hydrogen bomb). The committee gave the following advice, even though the USA's rival, the Soviet Union, had made an atomic bomb.

We base our recommendations on our belief that the extreme dangers to mankind inherent in the proposal wholly outweigh any military advantage that could come from this development. Let it be clearly realized that this is a superweapon; it is in a totally different category from an atomic bomb. The reason for developing such superbombs would be to have the capacity to devastate a vast area with a single bomb. Its use would involve a decision to slaughter a vast number of civilians. We are alarmed as to the possible global effects of the radioactivity generated by the explosion of a few superbombs of conceivable magnitude. If superbombs will work at all, there is no inherent limit in the destructive power that may be attained with them. Therefore a superbomb might become a weapon of genocide [the slaughter of entire peoples].

In 1968, a rally takes place in London to press for nuclear disarmament. It is addressed by Mashashi Nii, a terminally ill survivor of Hiroshima.

What have we learnt from Hiroshima?

Eyewitness accounts of decisions, events and sufferings help us to grasp the human reality of what happened at Hiroshima. It is much more difficult to disentangle the motives behind decisions and decide how justified they were – especially when we take into account the problems facing politicians, soldiers and scientists at the time.

One thing that Hiroshima and Nagasaki did for the world was to alert it to the horrors of nuclear war. Despite fierce conflicts, nuclear weapons have never been used since then – but the danger has not gone away.

The **Cold War** ended with the collapse of the **Soviet Union** in December 1991. A worldwide nuclear war had been avoided and the USA was left as the only superpower. But more states – Israel, India, Pakistan – had acquired nuclear weapons, and it seemed possible that others might sooner or later do so. In the 1990s and 2000s, unstable **dictators** and **terrorist** groups posed new threats. If any of these manage to make, buy or steal nuclear weapons, there could be terrible disasters. Such is the fearful legacy of Hiroshima and Nagasaki.

Lanterns floating on the Motoyasu River at Hiroshima commemorate the people killed by the **atomic bomb.**

The nuclear nightmare

A present-day writer, Robert Hutchinson, reflects gloomily on the continuing threat posed by nuclear weapons, along with biological and chemical weapons; all three are now known as WMD (weapons of mass destruction).

Come the end of the Cold War, triggered by the collapse of . . . the Soviet Union . . . there was an almost audible global sigh of relief that the bad old days . . . had wonderfully, miraculously gone for ever. 'Peace in our time!' was enthusiastically and universally proclaimed – this time, at least.

But peace and international security remained elusive. In reality the world has become a more uncertain and more dangerous place.

The nuclear genie cannot be squeezed back into the bottle. Only a feeble-minded politician would think otherwise. Today's reality is, in many ways, more frightening than the old East-West nuclear confrontation. Those who may arm themselves with the weapon of nuclear radioactivity today have radically different and more unpredictable motives than the member states of the 'nuclear club', who have developed their own nuclear weapons and are bound by some, at least, of the accepted diplomatic and political conventions.

Despite all our best hopes, the end of the nuclear nightmare was mere illusion. It should now loom larger in our daylight fears than ever it did in the latter, stable days of the Cold War.

Timeline

c.400 BC   The ancient Greek philosopher Democritus suggests that all **matter** is made up of atoms

c.1803   British scientist John Dalton establishes **atomic theory**

1905   Albert Einstein's mathematical formula for the conversion of **mass** into energy provides the basis for future nuclear physics

1931   The Japanese seize Manchuria

1933   Hitler takes power in Germany

1937   The Japanese invade China

1938   Hahn and Strassmann discover **nuclear fission**; their discovery is identified by Meitner and Frisch, and becomes widely known among scientists

1939   September: outbreak of World War II

October: US President Roosevelt receives a letter from Albert Einstein, urging US research into making an **atomic bomb**

1940-41   **Nazi** Germany conquers much of Europe

1941   June: Nazi Germany invades the **Soviet Union**

December: Japanese attack on Pearl Harbor; USA enters World War II; work intensifies on what becomes known as the Manhattan Project

1942   Working in the USA, Enrico Fermi constructs the first **nuclear reactor**

1945   April: Harry S Truman becomes US president

May: Germany surrenders, ending the war in Europe

July: Potsdam Conference between the **Allied** leaders; atomic bomb tested at Alamogordo; Truman authorizes use of the bomb

August: atomic bombs are dropped on Hiroshima and Nagasaki; Japan surrenders; end of World War II

1947   Worsening relations between USA and its allies and their wartime partner, the Soviet Union; the **Cold War** begins about this time

1951   Japan becomes independent again

1952   USA tests the first **hydrogen bomb**; the Soviet Union, Britain, China and France follow later

1960s   **ICBMs** are produced and stockpiled by both sides in the Cold War

1970s   Some agreements on nuclear weapons are reached by the USA and the Soviet Union; India, Pakistan and other nations develop, or are suspected of developing, nuclear weapons

1991   Break-up of the Soviet Union; the end of the Cold War

2001   Destruction of the World Trade Center, New York City, on 11 September – the most violent example of an upsurge of worldwide **terrorist** activity

2003   US 'war on terror' continues and the North Korean nuclear weapons programme causes concern

Find out more

Books & websites

Atoms, Chris Oxlade (Heinemann, 2002)

Eye-Witness Hiroshima, edited byAdrian Weale (Robinson, 1995)

Hiroshima, John Hersey (Penguin. Originally published in 1946; the 1985 edition carries the story further.)

Hiroshima, Jason Hook (Hodder Wayland, 2002)

Spotlight on the Second World War, Nathaniel Harris (Wayland, 1985)

Turning Points in History: Hiroshima: The Shadow of the Bomb, Richard Tames (Heinemann Library, 1999)

20th Century Perspectives: Weapons and Technology of World War II, Windsor Chorlton (Heinemann Library, 2002)

http://www.heinemannexplore.co.uk
Go Exploring! Log on to Heinemann's online history resource.

http://www.csi.ad.jp/hiroshima

http://www.mtholyoke.educ/acad/intrel/hiroshima.htm

List of primary sources

The author and publisher gratefully acknowledge the following publications and websites from which written sources in the book are drawn. In some cases the wording or sentence structure has been simplified to make the material more appropriate for a school readership.

P.9 From *What Little I Remember* by Otto R. Frisch (Cambridge University Press, 1979)

P.11 From *The Greatest Power on Earth* by Ronald W. Clark (Sidgwick and Jackson, 1980)

P.13 From *Bird of Passage: recollections of a physicist* by Rudolf Peierls (Princeton University Press, 1985)

P.15 The words of John Garcia, quoted by Studs Terkel in *The Good War: An Oral History of World War II* (Hamish Hamilton, 1985)

P.17 From *Now It Can Be Told* by Leslie R. Groves (Harper and Brothers, 1962)

P.19 The words of Brigadier General Thomas F. Farrell, whose account is reproduced in *Now It Can Be Told* by Leslie R. Groves (Harper and Brothers, 1962)

P.21 From the website Hiroshima, The Henry Stimson Diary and Papers (part 8). The diary and papers themselves are in the Henry Lewis Stimson Papers, Manuscripts and Archives, Yale University Library, New Haven, Connecticut, and also in the Library of Congress, Washington, DC, and the Center For Research Libraries, Chicago, IL.

P.23 From *Off the Record: The Private Papers of Harry S Truman* by Robert H. Ferrell (Harper and Row, 1980)

P.25 'Ike on Ike', *Newsweek* magazine, 11 November 1963; quoted in *The Nuclear Age* by John Newhouse (Michael Joseph, 1989)

P.27 Widely quoted, e.g. in *Eye-Witness Hiroshima* by Adrian Weale (ed.), (Robinson, 1995)

P.29 From *Cries for Peace: Experiences of Japanese Victims of World War II*, compiled by the Youth Division of Soka Gakkai (The Japan Times Ltd., 1978)

P.31 From *Cries for Peace: Experiences of Japanese Victims of World War II*, compiled by the Youth Division of Soka Gakkai (The Japan Times Ltd., 1978)

P.33 From an article by Gordon Walker in the *Observer* newspaper, 5 August 1945

P.35 From *Warrior Without Weapons* by Marcel Junod (Cape, 1951)

P.37 The words of Paul Fussell: quoted in *The Making of the Atomic Bomb* by Richard Rhodes (Penguin, 1988)

P.39 From the *New York Times* article of 9 September 1945 by William T. Laurence; reproduced in *The Faber Book of Reportage* (Faber, 1987)

P.41 Widely quoted, e.g. in *Eye-Witness Hiroshima* by Adrian Weale (ed.), (Robinson, 1995)

P.43 From *Cries for Peace: Experiences of Japanese Victims of World War II*, compiled by the Youth Division of Soka Gakkai (The Japan Times Ltd., 1978)

P.45 From *At the Barricades* by Wilfred Burchett (Quartet Books, 1980) (Burchett's article about radiation was published on 6 September 1945 in the *Daily Express* newspaper.)

P.47 From *Blundering into Disaster* by Robert McNamara (Bloomsbury, 1987)

P.49 From *The Greatest Power on Earth* by Ronald W. Clark (Sidgwick and Jackson, 1980)

P.51 From *Weapons of Mass Destruction* by Robert Hutchinson (Weidenfeld and Nicolson, 2003)

Glossary

alliance   agreement made by two or more countries to work or fight together against a present or future enemy

Allied   describes the Allies (see below)

Allies   states that fought against Germany and its partners in World Wars I and II. In both wars the Allies included Britain, France, Russia and the USA.

atomic bomb   bomb in which atomic particles are split, causing an enormous explosion

atomic particles   tiny units of which all matter is composed

atomic theory   study of the composition and behaviour of atoms

barium   chemical element (basic substance) that played a part in the discovery of nuclear fission

Cold War   name given to the hostility that existed between the free enterprise capitalist and communist worlds between 1947 and the late 1980s

colony   area of land where political power and natural resources are controlled by the government of another country

Cuban Missile Crisis   crisis that broke out in October 1962, when the USA discovered Soviet Russian missile sites on the island of Cuba; for a time, a nuclear war seemed likely

debriefed   servicemen and agents are debriefed immediately after a mission – they report and answer questions about what they have done or seen

democracy   political system in which governments are regularly elected by the mass of the people

dictator   an individual who has complete control of a state

electron   very light particle, found in atoms, which moves round the nucleus

gamma rays   type of radiation, similar to X-rays

Geiger counter   instrument used to detect and measure radiation

hydrogen bomb   type of bomb even more powerful than the atomic bomb; it was based on fusing rather than splitting atoms

ICBMs   Intercontinental Ballistic Missiles – missiles capable of crossing from one continent to another, carrying nuclear warheads

incendiary bombs   bombs containing materials that will burst into flames on impact and start fires in enemy territory

isotopes   different types of atom found in the same chemical element (basic substance)

kamikaze describes Japanese pilots or planes that flew suicide missions; the planes were intended to crash into enemy ships and sink them

mass a way of measuring matter – according to its resistance to change (inertia) when acted upon

matter material substance; everything in the visible Universe

Nazi Party political party, led by Adolf Hitler, that controlled Germany between 1933 and 1945

neutron particle found in the nucleus of an atom

neutron bomb small bomb that detonates with a minimal blast, limiting material damage; it sends out radiation more widely, killing people at a greater distance

New Mexico one of the states of the USA, in the southwest of the country

nuclear fission splitting the nucleus of an atom, an operation that releases enormous energy

nuclear reactor device used to achieve nuclear fission in a controlled (non-explosive) fashion

nucleus core of an atom; the plural (more than one nucleus) is nuclei

oral historian historian who specializes in recording people's spoken testimony

physicists experts in the science of physics

plutonium chemical element (basic substance) produced from uranium and used in creating nuclear energy

radium artificially produced radioactive material

Soviet Union or USSR – a state including but very much larger than present-day Russia. It was the ally of the USA in World War II, but later its opponent in the Cold War, until it collapsed in 1991.

terrorists individuals or groups who spread terror in a society through bombings, kidnappings etc., usually to achieve political or religious aims

uranium chemical element (basic substance) used to create nuclear energy

Index